the *American* Cinquain

poetry by

Sandy White

Finishing Line Press
Georgetown, Kentucky

the *American* Cinquain

TO THOSE PERSONS

*The ones
who love to make
other people laugh with
the Art of Laughter. You know who
you are.*

Copyright © 2025 by Sandy White
ISBN 979-8-89990-138-6 First Edition
All rights reserved under International and Pan-American Copyright Conventions. No part of this book may be reproduced in any manner whatsoever without written permission from the publisher, except in the case of brief quotations embodied in critical articles and reviews.

Publisher: Leah Huete de Maines
Editor: Christen Kincaid
Cover Art: : *The Crow*, soft pastel, Sandy White, sandywhitefineart.com
Author Photo: Nick White, nickwhitephotography.net
Cover Design: Elizabeth Maines McCleavy

Order online: www.finishinglinepress.com
also available on amazon.com

Author inquiries and mail orders:
Finishing Line Press
PO Box 1626
Georgetown, Kentucky 40324
USA

Contents

AN INVITATION WHEN YOU NEED ONE 1
ARRIVING LIKE ATHENA 2
THE ART CRITIC 3
AS THE CROW FLIES 4
AT NIGHT 5
BENEATH THE SCENE 6
BOTTOM FEEDER 7
BUCKING AROUND 8
CAMPING 9
COMFORT 10
COMING OF THE AGES 11
COMING TO TERMS 12
COURAGE 13
DEATH'S DISTANCE 14
A DREAM 15
DREAM OF THE RESURRECTION 16
A DROWNING 17
THE ECSTASY OF SINGING 18
ELECTRICAL 19
THE EXIT 20
FANTAIL PIGEONS 21
FAST, PAST, GONE 23
FULL OF WEEDS 24
GHOST POEM 25
GOING IT ALONE 26
HA HA HA 27
HIDDEN COSTS 28
HOW I LEARNED PATIENCE 29
THE HOWLING 30
THE HUG 31
IF I WERE A MAPLE TREE 32
I'LL GO 33
IN BED 34
I SAW 35

IT GOT ABSORBED	36
IT WON'T STAND STILL	37
JUST LIKE A BABY BIRD	38
LISTEN	39
LOST AND FOUND	40
LOVE STORY	41
MEMORY BANK: HALF EMPTY, HALF FULL	42
MOM WAS A TEXAN ON THE EAST COAST	43
MY LONG LIST	44
NIGHT OUT, ON CITY SIDEWALKS	45
ONENESS	46
THE PIPERS CALL	47
PLEASURES	48
THE POETRY PIXIES	49
PREPARATION	50
REINCARNATION	51
THE RIGHT RITE	52
THE SECRET HELPER	53
the sock	54
SOMETHING TO CARRY	55
SO MUCH FOR PLANNING	56
STAR GAZING	57
SUCCESSFUL SECRETS	58
TELL ME, WAS IT YOU?	59
THERAPY AT THE SCHOOL OF SORCERY	60
TOMORROW	61
TOUCH	62
TRUE MINDS	63
UNLOCKING LIFE	64
UROBOROS	65
THE VORACIOUS SHADOW	66
WAITING GAME	67
WALKING	68
WALKING IN THE FOREST	69
THE WEIGHT OF DUTY	70
WHAT I GOT OUT OF SCHOOL	71
THE WORD THAT GOT AWAY	72
WRITER'S BLOCK	73

In the early 1900s, Adelaide Crapsey invented a five-line short form of poetry now known as the American Cinquain, based partially on her study of Cherokee incantations.

Most readers of short forms are familiar with Japanese Haiku and Tonka, but few are familiar with Adelaide's home-grown American Cinquain.

DEFINITION

Cinquain:
story told in
twenty-two syllables,
five lines of 2-4-6-8-2.
That's it.

The following 72 American Cinquains are presented alphabetically.

AN INVITATION WHEN YOU NEED ONE

"Climb in
and sit awhile",
said the dryad. "It's just
a hollow tree. A place to hide.
Come in."

ARRIVING LIKE ATHENA

Certain
poems just don't
get finished, no matter
how many flings with a paper
and pen.

While some
other poems
loosen forth in grandness,
full-blown, as if from the forehead
of Zeus.

THE ART CRITIC

Placid
landscape painters
paint views as calm, restrained.
No-risk postcards for the paying
tourists.

The art
I love is on
the move, provocative
to my spirit. Nothing static
or safe.

Pollock
dances and drips
down house paint onto bare
canvas, pouring action down like
weather.

Van Gogh
swirls energy
like a scientist. He
paints atomic pathways, reaching
for stars.

Rembrandt
draws forth backlight
from behind his drawing.
Holy light. Gleaming through to kiss
his eyes.

AS THE CROW FLIES

The Scots
made this saying
from watching flying crows,
who flew the straightest course to find
their food.

Now you
and I straight talk
like hungry crows, seeking
the shortest route to a point, to
a truth.

AT NIGHT

I pour
forth words. My lips
confess unto your ears
the thoughts that hide inside my heart
all day.

All day,
those thoughts inside
my hidden heart, find words
to form into confessions for
your ears.

Your ears
wait for my lips
to fill you up with words.
My heart confesses to those thoughts
inside.

Inside,
my heart forms words
to pour into your ears.
My lips confess my hidden ways
all night.

BENEATH THE SCENE

Roots of
those big trees feel
deeply down into earth.
We can't see them holding hands, but
they do.

BOTTOM FEEDER

I look
for stuff floating
down for me to nibble;
thrift shop finds, used books, castaway
lovers.

BUCKING AROUND

Tying
words down is like
lassoing, then riding
words in a rodeo called a
poem.

CAMPING

A tent
covers over.
Wool blankets lay below.
Rain roars and pours. Our pillow falls
asleep.

COMFORT

like joy,
effervesces;
soothes, heals, loves and blesses
until it runs completely out
of verbs.

COMING OF THE AGES

They had
to run on out
of the doors, to meet their
glandular futures, just like all
the kids

from all
the centuries,
who leave through back or front
doors, hearing calls by orgasmic
pipers,

moving
towards their fates.
Ready. Magnetic. True.
As if the dance were different
this time.

COMING TO TERMS

A Lie
conversed with Truth.
They sought a covenant.
Each is the other inside out.
Both said.

COURAGE

Just take
it for a spin.
Check it out, notice how
it unfolds as you reach beyond
your reach.

DEATH'S DISTANCE

In the
corner of my
eye, a ladder reached down
as if to say, we're waiting for
you but

you won't
be climbing now.
This is a glimpse. Stay there
it told me, until you can see
an arm.

A DREAM

I land
on an island
where extinct volcanoes
spout forth and erupt, just like good
writing.

DREAM OF THE RESURRECTION

Somehow
the path out was
blocked, the old gate was locked.
Stones rolled in. Rocks climbed to the top
then stopped.

Somehow
a ladder crossed
over and raised me on
high, to fly with shiny new wings.
I flew

somehow,
landing on clouds
with no fear. Now I hear
happiness sing—and I'm smiling
out loud.

A DROWNING

The tears
that are not cried
well up so deep inside.
When tears are not cried out, most tears
won't leave.

THE ECSTASY OF SINGING

One note
made just for you
is all you get from God.
But when you hit it, you don't need
more notes.

ELECTRICAL

Barefoot,
we jitterbugged
with jagged lightning bolts,
flickering around the back yard
birdbath.

Wet sand
between our toes.
What would our mothers think
if we said we'd danced like little
witches.

THE EXIT

Pretend
you know the way
out of this big mess when
nobody does. Would you take me
with you?

FANTAIL PIGEONS

Their eggs
floated away
in the rain gutter; twigs,
straw, vanished. Their next nest was an
old box.

                      An old
                      man lived alone
                      with his new wife. His kids,
                      first wife, kept pigeons; he gave us
                      their birds.

The new
nest perched on our
air conditioner. Three
eggs hatched. One survived to live through
Summer.

                      The train
                      had not stopped. Their
                      car had stalled on the tracks.
                      The lone man watched as his bloodline
                      perished.

Summer.
The pigeons moved
into our garage. I
held my hand patiently out, full
of corn.

                      The man
                      lived alone with
                      his new wife. He'd given
                      pigeons from his kids and first wife
                      to us.

Autumn
came. They were tame.
Strutting about our yard,
they'd lost what survival fear they
would need.

                The man
                had watched her car
                stall on train tracks; the train
                could not stop. He watched his bloodline
                perish.

Winter
brought snow, blood red
drops, white feathers, icy
patches next to dark, melting, fox
paw marks.

                The man's
                bloodline perished.
                He'd watched the car stall on
                railroad tracks; the engineer could
                not stop.

FAST, PAST, GONE

I tried
to remember
the last time that something
lasted, but nothing lasted long
enough.

FULL OF WEEDS

Years gone.
A promise not
kept still echoes inside.
My heart grows like an abandoned
garden.

GHOST POEM

I wrote
a rhythm down
but watched as words vanished.
Dark words. Not ready to be heard.
Not yet.

GOING IT ALONE

Boxing
in the shadows
with nothing to sustain
me, except a far off sound of
music.

HA HA HA

Sorrow
flew in on wings
like a hawk. Happiness
refused to become its prey and
stayed put.

HIDDEN COSTS

I need
to file for a
permit to live as a
hermit, but permission isn't
that free.

The list
of expenses
charged to vexing my life
is too taxing for a hermit
like me.

HOW I LEARNED PATIENCE

Mud cakes.
Little berries.
Placed upon the threshold
of a tiny hut I'd built, made
of sticks.

I was
a giantess
waiting for glimpses of
spirits who frolicked through our
back yard.

THE HOWLING

Tangled
in snares and traps,
I listen for the wolf.
He's near. Soon he will help me to
escape.

THE HUG

Your soul's
temperature
encircles me. I had
forgotten just how warm your warmth
could be.

IF I WERE A MAPLE TREE

I would
melt to you all
the syrup I have stored
up. I wood drip and leak it all
to you.

I'LL GO

Freedom
arises from
my imagination
wanting to take me for a long,
long walk.

IN BED

You want
to look at me
with the lights on, but I
see your lights better when that light
is off.

I SAW

the light
behind the light
that makes the forest glow.
I know this light, that lights the light
then goes.

IT GOT ABSORBED

Something
drifted closer,
becoming a part of
everything else, then it could not
get back.

IT WON'T STAND STILL

Seek Truth.
It wanders far
from where you left it last.
The Truth is always on the move.
Look fast.

JUST LIKE A BABY BIRD

Hunger
lives inside each
one of us who hope for
God to poke a treat down into
our throats.

LISTEN

That tree
is talking to
those other trees—their roots
touch. My ear goes down to the ground
to hear.

LOST AND FOUND

I'm lost.
I cannot find
my way that went away,
perhaps because this other way
got found.

LOVE STORY

A bear
climbed up a tree.
I love its fur and nose.
Its eyes and claws and paws. It loves
its life.

The bear
cannot be my
friend. It will not love me
like you do, yet it carries me
away.

Far, far
away. Into
a world filled full of bears.
I cannot be a bear. I can
love you.

MEMORY BANK: HALF EMPTY, HALF FULL

One old
memory meant
too much to go away.
Another never meant enough
to stay.

MOM WAS A TEXAN ON THE EAST COAST

When I
pull out the weeds
from hard ground, I just say
'Howdy, Mom.' She tore weeds out by
deep roots.

What does
Aunt Viola
have against weeds, cousin
Dennis asked. She yanks them with such
fury.

She was
jumpy, I said,
as if she were a weed
herself, not wanting the whole world
to know.

MY LONG LIST

Count five
things I have learned?
Instead I start to list
the many things I know I've not
learned yet.

NIGHT OUT, ON CITY SIDEWALKS

Walking
sideways in the
night, I feel like a crab
who got lost far away from the
ocean.

ONENESS

Alone.
Even nature
does not distract my soul.
When by myself, I'm by myself.
Alone.

THE PIPERS CALL

Engines,
with sounds of songs
purring through exhaust pipes,
transporting love calls from suitors.
Menfolk

cruising
my way, revving
motorcycles, sports cars.
Vibrant rumblings vroooomed with no end.
But then,

these days
those songs aren't sung.
Another walks softly,
whistling close behind for a date,
and waits.

PLEASURES

An elf,
before I was
born, hid messages just
for me—wise puzzles, odd treasures,
under

deep dark
spaces that have
no map. I grab and stuff
my pockets full. Elves work with time
constraints

and there's
lots of hiding
for them to do so I
must solidify these gifts or
they'll melt.

THE POETRY PIXIES

Words don't
throw sparks today.
Pixies are holding up
an opaque sheet of plexi-glass.
I can't

look through
to see crystal
forests and words in streams.
Verse can't be transcribed when pixies
do this.

PREPARATION

Wearing
homemade costumes,
my dolls gave me a chance
to try on all the colors of
my Self.

Digging
in the dirt, my
shovel formed escape routes
so dolls could drive their cars on out
of town.

REINCARNATION

Old lives,
reaching into
this life, tease and toss their
weight around, asking me to take
them back.

THE RIGHT RITE

My foot
moves before my
tongue. Lips part. My throat flings
songs to anyone who dances.
Catch them.

THE SECRET HELPER

I saw
a transparent
charioteer guiding
four horses. "Just hop on board", he
told me.

"We won
the race. You hold
the olive branch. We did
this together, you and me, here's
your crown."

for Bobby

the sock

missing
from the bureau
drawer, its partner alone
inside, the other socks entwine
with mates

SOMETHING TO CARRY

Lanterns
inspire mental
quickness, emotional
calmness. A sense of mystery.
A search

for all
that might be met,
that might be beckoning
with one more step closer, holding
a light.

SO MUCH FOR PLANNING

A Squirrel
buries peanuts
in a hole for later.
The Crow looks on, then digs them up
for lunch.

STAR GAZING: you don't need us

I reached
for my star but
never caught what I'd sought.
Can't hitch my wagon to it. Can't
find it.

Although
a strange star I'd
seen when searching, just beamed
a twinkle down to me as if
to say:

Sorry,
we've been rather
busy up here. We know
you have much light to give but we're
just stars.

So, keep
on with those dreams.
You'll find yourself nearby.
Not in the sky. Feel deep. Look in.
Walk wide.

A SUCCESSFUL SECRET

is like
an oyster shell
clamping around a pearl
tightly, so it will never crack
open.

TELL ME, WAS IT YOU?

A kiss
from a dream fell
smack onto my waking
lips. Not knowing who was there, I
kissed back.

THERAPY AT THE SCHOOL OF SORCERY

Feckless
magicians waved
magic wands; but their spells
drooped, not divining on cue like
charms should.

Changing
incantations
did not enchant. Doctors
advised: put faith back into your
magic.

TOMORROW

Although
I haven't been
there yet: remembering
before I get there makes me want
to go.

TOUCH

Caress,
as if a reach
towards some blessed place
is nearer than you ever would
have thought.

TRUE MINDS

Certain
links cannot be
broken. Though seeming as
if they are torn asunder, they
are not.

UNLOCKING LIFE

I knock
on your doorway
if only in my mind.
Are you at home? Can you come out
to play?

UROBORUS

Built in
to beginnings
are endings, just waiting
for their turns to come so they can
begin.

THE VORACIOUS SHADOW

The beast
of the village
lurks in darkness, not light;
wolfish, devouring secrets
all night.

WAITING GAME

Titles
float by on their
magic carpets, to check
if I have finished writing my
poem.

Looking
to see if I
am ready for them yet.
Whether they should show up now or
later.

WALKING

That bird's
chirp caused me to
step from this path towards
a place I had not intended
to go.

WALKING IN THE FOREST

Green leaves
remind me of
spies who are secretly
watching, listening to all the ways
I move.

Soft leaves
brush across my
cheeks, my ears, telling me
what they know, glad that I am here.
I smile.

One leaf
flirts and tickles;
a chosen messenger
confirming that all life does love
the same.

THE WEIGHT OF DUTY

Lifting
an object with
thoughts attached to it can
make it heavier than it needs
to be.

WHAT I GOT OUT OF SCHOOL

I learned:
memorizing
took up space in my brain
and imagination wanted
that spot.

THE WORD THAT GOT AWAY

Not a
bird but a word
flew nearby. I caught it.
Another close behind, I grabbed
but missed.

WRITER'S BLOCK

There are
too many plum
blossoms floating by my
eyes, my nose, for me to write this
poem.

ACKNOWLEDGMENTS

The American Dissident, #44 Fall 2022
          FAST, PAST, GONE
          WHAT I GOT OUT OF SCHOOL
            #46 Fall 2023
          AS THE CROW FLIES
            #47 Spring 2024
          DREAM OF THE RESURRECTION
          HIDDEN COSTS
          UNLOCKING LIFE
          UROBOROS
            #48 Fall 2024
          TRUE MINDS
            #49 Spring 2025
          THE ART CRITIC

Marin Poetry Center online newletter
          CAMPING
          DEATH'S DISTANCE
          THE ECSTASY OF SINGING
          FAST, PAST, GONE
          IF I WERE A MAPLE TREE
          I SAW
          IT WON'T STAND STILL
          MY LONG LIST
          SO MUCH FOR PLANNING
          TELL ME, WAS IT YOU?
          THE WORD THAT GOT AWAY

Marin Poetry Center 2025 Anthology
          DREAM OF THE RESURRECTION

NonBinary Review #29, Zoetic Press
          WALKING

Word Wranglers of West Marin, a Poetry Anthology
          AT NIGHT
          BENEATH THE SCENE
          THE ECSTASY OF SINGING
          IN BED

JUST SAYIN'

These are
not Japanese
Haiku or Japanese
Tanka. They are American
Cinquain.

Sandy White spent most of her early years nestled in a very old, thick-walled stone house in the hilly country of Landenberg, Pennsylvania. There weren't too many people around to play with, so nature and animals became companions. Stray dogs, cats, salamanders, turtles, pigeons, parakeets and numerous trees and a special boulder were all intimate friends with languages of their own. Then off to private day school in Delaware, beginning first grade at the age of four. With little socialization, always being behind or ahead, there was little else for her to do than to eventually become an artist of some kind. A high school art teacher pointed one way and she received a BFA in Painting from the University of Pennsylvania in conjunction with the Pennsylvania Academy of the Fine Arts in Philadelphia. Her website for pastels and painting is: www.sandywhitefineart.com

A high school English teacher had also tugged at the edges of her imagination and championed her towards story telling in theater and in verse, which finally culminated in a late-life MFA in Creative Writing/Poetry at Dominican University of California in 2022. While at Dominican, Sandy, who has always gravitated towards the little-known, the hidden, the unpopular and the rare, discovered Adelaide Crapsey and her early 1900s invention of the American Cinquain. In no time at all, Sandy realized that no educated person she talked to had ever heard of Adelaide Crapsey or her short form of poem. The next step was to learn how to write one, eventually modernizing the form with an occasional use of stanzas. The first cinquain took all day to write. Then came along the second, then the third …

www.ingramcontent.com/pod-product-compliance
Lightning Source LLC
Chambersburg PA
CBHW030055170426
43197CB00010B/1540